Contents

1 Introduction

Risk is an inherent part of child placement practice. The multiple and complex needs of those children requiring permanent care mean that the resources of families, social workers and agencies all need to combine in order to ensure that the potential for positive outcomes is maximised. Government initiatives to raise standards of agency practice along with an increasing awareness of the numbers of children who might benefit from adoption are to be welcomed. However, there is a danger of an over-emphasis on statistics and targets without a corresponding commitment to assessing individual needs and recognising the quality of work which is essential to making good placements.

There are a number of key stages in placing children for adoption, each of which has its own particular challenges. Planning, working with both child and birth family, preparing and assessing applicants are all areas that demand intensive, skilled and focused work. This is recognised and reflected in the variety of written material which exists in order to help practitioners and families think about different aspects of the task (see Resources, p.20).

In contrast, the vital phase of linking children with new families and introducing them to each other prior to placement has received little attention within social work literature. This practice guide is an attempt to fill that gap and to provide social workers – particularly those with limited experience of family placement – with a possible framework for thinking through the major stages of linking and introducing.

It is founded on the principle of the needs of the child being paramount and that this should be reflected in all decisions, plans and actions. Similarly, it underlines the importance of proactively working with children, consulting them and listening to them in order to meet their needs effectively. The text draws on a variety of sources including BAAF's earlier publication on disruption (Smith, 1994) and integrates current assessment material produced by the Department of Health with recent research findings that have particular relevance for practice.

In order to establish workable parameters, this guide starts from the point when a child is identified as needing adoption and social workers are at the point of considering resources. While the primary focus is adoption, the underlying principles and practice issues are equally relevant to any placement which is intended to provide long-term stability for children. The text first considers issues related to linking children with potential families and explores the challenge of assessing needs and strengths as well as balancing and minimising risk. It then looks at the period of preparation prior to the first meeting when all involved begin to deal with the reality of impending introductions. Finally, it deals with aspects of the introductory process and comments on the different stages that build on each other to create a firm foundation for the placement. Current research is referenced throughout and practice tools, drawn largely from existing agency materials, are reproduced or referenced in the Tools Section.

2 Linking

Understanding children's needs

Understanding children, their history and its impact, their attachments, behaviours and functioning are all critical aspects of assessment. There is consistent evidence from both research and practice that in addition to age, a number of factors relating to children's past and present experience can affect successful placement outcome (Thoburn *et al*, 1999; Quinton *et al*, 1998; Lowe *et al*, 1999). These variables include the level of deprivation and/or abuse; the quality of early attachments; the number of moves prior to placement; the current level of emotional/behavioural functioning; and whether or not the child has been separated from a sibling.

Yet disruption experience and research (Lowe *et al*, 1999; Quinton *et al*, 1998) continue to report that too often children are placed without a detailed and accurate assessment of their experience and needs as the basis for discussion and decision making. There are some circumstances when, despite every effort, the quality of information available may be limited, but at the very least, gaps should be explored and acknowledged before engaging with potential families. The requirement to collate, assess and convey such crucial information is imperative both for the child and his/her new family. Agencies may wish to review how they maintain systems and recording procedures that ensure the availability and accessibility of key information relating to children, perhaps in summary form or with the use of visual aids such as flow charts, geneograms, etc.

What then are some of the key areas of assessment that a social worker will need to explore before feeling confident about considering appropriate family resources? What is recent research telling us about specific areas of risk that may require more careful consideration at this stage? While individual agencies may have their own assessment formats, childcare staff will hopefully be familiar with the assessment diagram reproduced in the recent *Framework for the Assessment of Children in Need and their Families* (DoH, 2000). This can help to provide a comprehensive and holistic picture of a child's developmental needs within the context of parenting, family and environmental factors (see Tool 3). It can increase understanding of a child's birth family experience as well as highlighting issues about the adoptive family that will require particular consideration in the light of previous patterns or unmet needs.

Romanian research (Rutter *et al*, 1998) indicates that it is the duration of deprivation rather than its severity that seems more likely to affect recovery. This confirms the urgency of clear, purposeful planning and the avoidance of undue delay. These are important factors in working both with birth families and foster carers. Too often children linger in temporary care and decisions about permanence are then far harder and more complicated. Lowe *et al* (1999) draw attention to the added risks incurred by breaking settled attachments that children have established with existing carers. Sometimes there are valid reasons for moving children on but it is necessary to be clear about when and why this is genuinely in the child's interests.

In addition, research indicates other potentially important factors about children that may need more careful scrutiny prior to linking. The study by Quinton *et al* (1998) suggests that certain groups of children may be at particular risk. These include children who were rejected or scapegoated by their parent(s) – especially when other siblings remained at home – and children who are unusually overactive and restless. Lowe *et al* (1999) identify violent or sexually abusive behaviour towards other children as being another high-risk indicator. However, it is important to note that these factors cannot be seen in isolation and the research emphasises that it is the way in which the needs of children combine and interact with the nature of the family resources (see "Considering resources" below) that seems to increase the level of risk.

Making sense of children's needs is not easy and involves not just assembling facts but understanding family experience, observing, listening and communicating. Sadly, there are an increasing number of children who have had very traumatic pasts and who subsequently have major difficulties with attachments, self-esteem, and managing their behaviour. It is not unusual for less experienced social workers to feel overwhelmed by the depth of need presented by such children and good supervision/consultation as well as liaison with family placement teams is often helpful in order to reach a clear and evidenced assessment. This will be essential both for panel presentation and as a basis for discussion with potential families. At this stage all involved have an understandable desire to look positively to the future. Children often make marked progress in short-term care and the tendency to over-emphasise this at the expense of minimising the impact of early deprivation/trauma is dangerous. But it is also important to remember that children who have experienced pain and trauma will have developed defensive strategies in order to survive. When these areas are recognised and discussed, new parents can begin to understand behaviour in the light of experience and help the child to work on their strengths while letting go of underlying fears. But this is no easy task and it will be important for all concerned to be realistic in recognising that long-term and persistent trauma can result in behaviours that are both challenging to live with and resistant to change.

Siblings

Many children in public care are part of a sibling group. Some will have siblings who remain in the family home; some will be living with their siblings and others will have siblings who are also looked after but placed in separate foster homes. Decisions about placement for siblings are often complex and it is easy, even within relationships where there are stresses and tensions, to underestimate the vital connections that siblings provide for each other. Research (Wedge and Mantle, 1991) indicates that too often siblings are separated on the basis of little evidence about the quality of their interaction. Decisions are more likely to be influenced by perceived individual needs, finance, different ages and heritages, and most frequently by availability of resources.

More recent research (Lowe et al, 1999) confirms previous findings that splitting siblings who had been part of a family group increases the risk of a poor outcome. Yet many siblings are separated once they come into the public care system, not in a planned way but purely because of availability of resources. It is therefore important not only to

increase resources to enable siblings to remain together but also to exercise caution in reaching conclusions about separation without appropriate evidence. Sometimes there are good reasons why siblings need to be separated, such as when dysfunctional family patterns are repeatedly played out and this inhibits both emotional growth and recovery. However, decisions to separate have to be evidenced by observation and assessment over time and children's wishes and feelings need to be heard and worked with. This is harder to achieve when separate placements are involved and proactive efforts to promote and observe contact as well as supporting the individual child are crucial.

Defining who is a sibling is also a complex question. Some children may have spent more of their life with fostered or adopted siblings than their biological family members. Again, the value of listening to children and understanding their perception of their important connections is underlined. For more detailed guidance about placing siblings see the BAAF Practice Guide *Together or Apart? Assessing brothers and sisters for permanent placement* (Lord and Borthwick, forthcoming 2001) and *We Are Family* (Mullender, 1999).

Wishes and feelings

Listening to children's wishes and feelings is an acknowledged aspect of assessment but needs to be seen in context. It is clearly essential to listen to what children think and feel about their situation, and direct work skills are crucial, especially with pre-verbal and/or disabled children. Research is now telling us far more about the concerns and worries that children have at this stage of their lives. They have views about their racial, cultural and religious origins, contact, education; about the kind of family they would like to live with; and about the qualities they value in prospective parents. They want to understand and make sense of their history and be involved in plans for their future (Thomas et al, 1999; Owen, 1999; Thoburn et al, 1999). So, communicating with children and giving them the opportunity to feel heard and respected is an important part of assessing their needs. Some children will find great difficulty in expressing their wishes and feelings and need time in which to build a relationship of trust within which they feel safe enough to express themselves.

However, decision making is the responsibility of adults and it is always necessary to put the wishes and feelings of children into a wider context. For example, some children of black or mixed parentage are confused about their identity as a result of their history and have internalised racist attitudes that will profoundly impact upon their view of themselves and their world. Others will be so fearful or vulnerable following abuse/emotional neglect that they may find it almost impossible to take the risk of being in touch with and expressing their true feelings (see Schofield, 1998). This can take the form of idealisation, refusal to engage or make choices, over-compliance or outright hostility. While it is essential to communicate with children, it is equally important to bear in mind their history, experience and emotional development in order that informed decisions about their future might be made.

Considering resources

Some of the most challenging messages from recent adoption research are in the area of considering resources. Availability of families for those children waiting for placement remains a genuine concern, yet evidence suggests that applicants – and children – continue to be disadvantaged by the prejudices of those with responsibility for decision making. Thus, Owen (1999) points out that single applicants were often viewed as a placement of last resort although the successful outcome of her study sample, albeit small, is remarkable. Lowe *et al* (1999) refer to variable policies regarding age, working mothers and infertility treatment. Similarly, agency attitudes were mixed about foster carers adopting. Yet their research shows that children already attached to a carer did well when adopted and that breaking settled attachments was an added risk factor. But some of the most significant messages to emerge from research around linking and matching relate to the interplay between the characteristics of the child, as mentioned above, household composition and parenting style.

In the past, social workers have often tended to prefer experienced parents for children with emotional difficulties. It was thought that real experience of raising children together with having had parental needs met by birth children might result in more confident parenting, but without undue emotional expectations. But current research (Quinton *et al*, 1998) challenges these long-held

assumptions, especially in relation to children with certain characteristics, e.g. those rejected or scapegoated; those placed alone without siblings; and those with overactive behaviours. The risks for these children appear to increase when they are placed with experienced parents with "own" children and such parents tended to be less warm and responsive towards the placed child. This echoes earlier child protection research (Dartington Social Research Unit, 1995) that highlighted the importance of a "high warmth – low criticism" environment for particularly vulnerable children. Interestingly, Owen's (1999) study suggests that the presence in the family of another *adopted* child, when well spaced, was a protective factor.

While this is a complex picture that by no means negates the contribution of experienced parents as adopters, there are potentially important lessons. Perhaps the over-riding message is that traditional assumptions about "ideal" placements may be questionable. Careful assessment is required that details an individual child's experience and needs and considers these in relation to the parenting style of potential applicants and the composition of their household.

These research findings raise interesting questions around assessment of families wanting to adopt children with special needs. How do we assess and evidence warmth and responsiveness? What safeguards can be built in to the assessment process to ensure that the added risks to existing children in the family are more clearly addressed?

The views of children about possible new families

Children have many views about the qualities, age, skills and composition of their new families yet rarely feel heard or involved (Thomas *et al*, 1999). They also have real concerns about contact with their family of origin, especially siblings that are being placed separately. The waiting period between the plan for permanence and linking with a specific family is often experienced as long and stressful and children develop different ways of managing their anxiety. Their views emphasise the importance of ongoing communication with and support for children throughout the placement process. Achieving placements does sometimes take far longer than originally envisaged and often it is the adult's sense of powerlessness and frustration that inhibits open discussion with the child. Children need to be free to employ their own defensive strategies in the face of stress. But it is also important that social workers and carers are communicating with them appropriately throughout this difficult phase and offering emotional reassurance and support.

Research is also beginning to provide more qualitative information about the experience of black and minority ethnic children in transracial placements (Thoburn et al, 1999; Kirton and Woodger, 1999). Black young people who were placed in white families, while affirming the many positive experiences of their placements, acknowledge the advantages of placement with a family of the same ethnicity. Research data confirm that parents of a different ethnic origin have additional issues to face in helping their children develop a positive sense of their identity, establish meaningful connections within the black community and deal effectively with racism. This adds weight to the Children Act ethos and more recent guidance that 'Placement with a family of similar ethnic origin and religion is very often most likely to meet the child's needs as fully as possible...' (DoH, LAC (98) 20 1998). In the exceptional situations where this may not be possible, these key issues indicated by research are clearly vital to address in detail with potential family resources.

Fortunately, children do not always share adult prejudices about difference and diversity and it is hoped that professional views about "ideal" families are changing. Recent research (Owen, 1999) demonstrates that single parent adoption has positive outcomes and can offer some children with exceptional needs the best opportunity of family life. Certain groups of children seemed to gain particular benefit, such as girls who had been sexually abused and children who had previously experienced severe conflict and dispute between adult carers. Most of the children in the study saw distinct advantages in being parented by a single carer. For them there was no stigma attached to living with a single carer; their sense of being "different" related to their adopted status and early experience rather than to the structure of their adoptive family.

Assessing risks and making decisions

Every family resource will have its own strengths and vulnerable areas and every placement will have its

risks. Acknowledging these is the key to planning a placement that is child centred but which recognises the needs of the family and seeks to actively support and promote mutual understanding, attachments and commitment. Assessing strengths and risks is an integral part of placement planning and requires a structured approach to decision making which allows the agency to explore the issues objectively and openly.

Adoption panels are required to make a recommendation regarding the suitability of a family for a particular child and this is subsequently confirmed by the Agency decision-maker (see Lord et al, 2000). When there are choices to be made between more than one family, many agencies present only the final choice to their Panel. It is therefore especially important that earlier decisions are not made solely by the child's social worker with their manager, and that the agency and panel take wider responsibility for ensuring that choice is exercised fairly and in the best interests of the child and potential families. Most agencies convene a matching meeting at some stage of their placement process and bring together a range of people, some of whom are not directly involved with the child/family, to discuss the viability of a proposed placement.

There are a wide variety of linking forms used by social workers and panels (see Tools for examples). Whatever the format, it is helpful for workers and panel members to have a tool that can succinctly convey the needs of a child alongside the strengths and vulnerable areas of a potential family. This in turn can alert them to issues that require attention in terms of contingency planning and post placement support. In some agencies a matrix framework is used to assess risk (see Phillips and McWilliam, 1996) and the more evidenced approach, which has been introduced within the new Form F, will provide another overview of what applicants can offer in the light of individual needs.

Some panels invite adopters to be present when linking recommendations are made. This can be a useful way of ensuring that information is openly shared, as well as actively modelling a partnership approach towards achieving family life for our most vulnerable children. Others invite consenting birth parents to meet with panel representatives and share their hopes for their child's future. Some do both. The involvement and support of birth relatives can make all the difference to a successful placement and, where appropriate, can enable the child to make a smoother transition to his or her new family.

Taking risks will always be a part of child placement. The agency's responsibility is to be aware of those risks, weigh them carefully in terms of the cost to both child and family and do what it can to minimise them. This may involve consideration of a number of options, for example, extra financial or practical help; special medical or educational liaison; or access to therapeutic resources, etc. Some agencies use written Adoption Placement Plans, Contact Plans and Post-Adoption Agreements to address these issues in a more formalised way. What is important is that these aspects are considered and put in place prior to placement rather than later when the level of stress can be such that additional support is often perceived as being too little, too late.

Linking – summary

- Understand the needs of your child(ren) as thoroughly as possible, especially the impact of early experience on their development.

- Listen to children's wishes and feelings and involve them appropriately in the process.

- Consider the child's significant connections alongside the family's capacity to support them.

- Be careful not to become problem focused – identify strengths and coping strategies that can be used positively.

- Keep an open mind about the type of family that might best meet the child's needs.

- When considering resources, bear in mind potential added risks for children with certain characteristics.

- Consider evidence about parenting style and impact of household composition.

- Assess strengths and risks of potential resources and ensure adequate and collaborative decision making.

- Identify potential support services required to minimise risk.

3 Preparation

The child

A valuable contribution of recent and ongoing research is that the views of children are being heard and acknowledged. They talk of the anxiety of being adopted by strangers; of their wish to be involved in decisions and given information; of how they want help to make sense of past, present and future (Lowe *et al*, 1999). Good preparation for placement will be part of a far broader context of direct work that ideally will be available to the child throughout their time in public care. Before they are able to look to the future and contemplate taking risks with new relationships, children need time and help to make sense of why they are unable to live with their birth families. The feelings associated with separation are powerful, and direct work can provide the opportunity to address the mixed and complex emotions associated with loss, abuse and/or neglect. In the same way, some birth parents and/or relatives can play an invaluable role in helping children make sense of their past and giving permission for them to move on. Because of the deep feelings involved, most will need support to do so and individual work with them, perhaps by an independent person, can be beneficial for all parties. When parents or family members feel heard and affirmed, they can often play a key role in enabling the child to integrate their past, present and future.

Disabled and pre-verbal children frequently receive little if any preparatory work, often because their capacity to make sense of information and to express themselves is grossly underestimated. Recent studies (Lowe *et al*, 1999; Quinton *et al*, 1998) confirm the variable quality of direct work and highlight the importance of ensuring time and skill for effective communication with children. Factors such as training, confidence and availability contributed towards a better service but some children – those who were overactive or restless – were not responsive even to direct work of high quality. Again, individual assessment of needs is necessary in order to plan, co-ordinate and review how best to prepare each child for a new placement. There is a variety of literature available about communicating with children including materials and books that can be used in direct work – see relevant references in Resources, p.20.

Research (Lowe *et al*, 1999) highlights the role and contribution of existing carers in helping children move, suggesting that good preparation by carers can minimise risk. This raises questions for agencies about how foster carers are best helped to develop direct work skills so that they can actively support children to make positive transitions. In addition to clear purposeful planning and ongoing reviews, carers will need training opportunities as well as individual emotional support for themselves and their family.

The views of children

Children have also used some recent research projects to convey their feelings about the preparatory work that is undertaken with them (Thomas *et al*, 1999). They talked about the anxiety and fear that is an inevitable part of waiting to join a new family and facing the unknown. They found the concept of adoption difficult to make sense of and needed ongoing and repeated explanation. The majority of those children in the study who had life story books found them helpful, especially in terms of understanding their history. However, the number of children without such a book highlights variable practice. Life story books are by no means a panacea – indeed they can sometimes be relegated to little more than photograph albums. Yet children want and need avenues whereby they can begin to make sense of who they are and what has happened to them in order that they can move on emotionally. Too many remain in confusion and without having the opportunity to make sense of past and present before contemplating the future.

As well as reassurance from social workers and carers, children wanted to know as much as possible about the family they would be joining and appreciated visual aids such as family books, videos and photos. They were keen to understand more about family members, the family home, lifestyle and locality, and the new school, but also to share information about themselves. They wanted to talk about their likes and dislikes, hopes and fears, their past, and their feelings about contact. But few felt included in the process of conveying information about them and their history to their new family. Good direct work can be a useful tool in producing a variety of materials that lend themselves to sharing aspects of a child's story. Opportunities, as well as appropriate support, for children to think about what and how they would like to tell potential families about themselves are part of ongoing preparation.

Feelings of sadness and loss about birth relatives, current carers and existing connections are an inevitably painful part of preparing to move, however committed the child is to the long-term plan. Children's comments in the research indicate something of the immense strain involved in letting go of the familiar and venturing into the unknown. When so many have already experienced considerable trauma in their lives, it is salutary to think about the level of trust they are expected to place in others at this vulnerable time. An awareness of how stressful and fearful this phase may be for the child will ensure that planning constantly remains child focused and that support for the child is reviewed on an ongoing basis.

Presenting to the adopters

The stage at which social workers engage with families to discuss specific children and their needs is a crucial milestone in the linking process. For applicants this is often the culmination of many months, even years, of thinking about and preparing for placement. Now, a real child is in view and there are inevitably many emotions to manage and acknowledge. For the child's worker, discussion with a particular family signals what is hopefully the final stage of what may have been a long and frustrating placement process but with all the accompanying anxiety about the outcome. Some face-to-face discussion often takes place in advance of the decision making process, such as applicants being approached prior to panel in order to ascertain their interest in a specific child. Whatever the timing, the way in which information is presented and applicants supported is crucial. Relationships between workers and families built on openness, mutual respect, sensitivity and collaboration can only increase the likelihood of a successful placement. Applicants have the right to be valued rather than feel they have to convince the child's worker that they have something to offer. With their agency they have worked at reflection, learning and self-assessment throughout the preparation and approval process and the outcome should be summarised and evidenced within their Form F. The role of the child's social worker at this stage is not to covertly re-approve but to share as much as possible about the child's profile and to discuss this in

the light of the family's strengths and vulnerable areas. Following a period of reflection, those involved should then be clearer about whether or not to proceed.

The importance of full and accurate information about a child's history and needs has been mentioned previously, and research confirms that a significant proportion of families continue to feel dissatisfied with the quality of information given to them (Lowe *et al*, 1999; Quinton *et al*, 1998). Specific concerns were around the child's background and its impact, the emotional/behavioural profile; much was out of date, medical information was often deficient (especially regarding mental health and genetic risk) and sometimes the lack of current history and daily routines. While acknowledging that there are sometimes good reasons why detailed information is hard to obtain, it is essential that whatever is available should be conveyed in full and that it is up to date. Families cannot begin to make informed decisions about their capacity to parent a child and sustain a placement unless they are equipped to do so. A thorough, carefully shared assessment, full discussion with adults who know the child well, meeting significant family members and friends, and of course engaging with the child, will all help to make real the unique needs which the family will want to consider. Similarly, access to relevant sections of the child's file, reading Assessment and Action Records and thinking around different tools used by current carers and/or parents (see Questionnaires in DoH Assessment Framework material, 2000) can also stimulate the thinking of potential families about the rewards and challenges that may lie ahead.

Children's backgrounds are part of who they are and need to be conveyed sensitively and respectfully. Language is important and how we describe people and circumstances can influence attitudes. Controversial information is never easy and it is important to be clear about what can and cannot be evidenced. Attachment patterns can help us to understand behaviour and responses and making sense of early experience and its impact is a crucial part of explaining needs. But children will have developed a range of strengths in order to survive previous hurt and it is important to draw these out along with their natural talents, aptitudes and interests. Visual aids such as photos, life books, videos, flow charts, eco maps, etc can all help to enlarge understanding of a child's world just as they can help the child to learn something of the new family and their lifestyle.

It is important to ensure not only that information is conveyed but that it is heard and understood, and that opportunities follow for reflection and discussion. One of the dangers at this point is that once families express an interest in a child the introductory process can follow almost immediately. The enthusiasm of the family and sometimes the social workers is understandable but taking the time to think and share can pay dividends. Much information is conveyed orally to families (Lowe et al, 1999) but it is useful to employ a variety of tools to communicate difficult and complex information in ways that families can make use of. Written information, visual aids, child appreciation meetings, and opportunities for individual consultations with health/education staff, are all additional ways of helping families think more realistically about needs and their ability to meet them.

Some agencies organise a more detailed and intensive meeting that might involve birth family members, potential adopters and professionals. This enables the child's story to be shared in considerable detail so that those present can reach a common understanding of the child's experience and needs. While at first sight this may appear to be costly in terms of time and resources, the investment can prove to be an invaluable building block. It allows information – including concerns – to be openly exchanged and discussed; it can empower adopters to listen, learn, ask questions and be thoroughly informed before making a commitment to proceed; and it helps birth relatives to feel included, valued and encouraged to play their part in planning for their child (see Tool 7: Information on child appreciation days).

Involving the family

A recurring message from research over the years – and repeated in recent studies – has been the increased risk of placing children close in age to existing children in the family. Findings about the advisability of placing children with certain characteristics within established families (Quinton et al, 1998) underline the importance of adequate preparation of the whole family group. Yet the studies (Lowe et al, 1999; Quinton et al, 1998) suggest a wide variation in the level of preparation, with parents themselves often left to undertake the task. While it is expected that most parents will want to prepare their own children, the agency also has a responsibility to ensure that the whole family is aware of the impact that a vulnerable child will have on their existing routines and relationships. Tackling these issues in a more rounded way might involve group work with existing children, involving them more explicitly in the preparation process and/or incorporating a systemic approach to family sessions (see *Making Good Assessments*, BAAF, 1999).

Similarly, the level of informal support provided by extended family and friends is noted in recent studies (Lowe et al, 1999; Owen, 1999) and practice experience confirms the value of existing networks in sustaining families through difficult times. However, the reverse is also true: that when anticipated informal support diminishes for whatever reason, the stress on family and child relationships can be heightened. This reminds us that families cannot be seen in isolation and that their capacity to work with others and to locate and use help when necessary are important aspects of their preparation and assessment. It may therefore be necessary for agencies to think more broadly about their preparation process in order to ensure that they, with their families, have the opportunity to genuinely explore the impact of placement within a wider kinship/friendship network.

Preparation – summary

- Ensure that direct work is well underway prior to linking so that communication and sharing throughout introductions follows naturally.

- Plan with the new family's worker how best to present information about the child's needs; provide an early opportunity to meet with significant people.

- Discuss carefully with current carers and their social worker who will be supporting the child emotionally throughout introductions.

- Remember that foster carers and their families will need ongoing support of their own in order to share their own feelings and help the child.

- Value and respect the particular skills and experiences of adoptive families.

- Don't be pressurised into hasty action. Allow time after initial discussion for reflection by all parties and give permission for doubts to be shared.

- Where possible, involve birth relatives in choice, meeting, exchanging information, etc, sooner rather than later.

- Be sure not to overlook existing children in the new family – they need to be involved.

4 Introductions

Planning

Planning meetings are an essential part of ensuring that introductions proceed as smoothly as possible. This is the opportunity for those involved to agree a framework for the various meetings, discussions and contacts that will aim to enable new relationships to slowly develop, and for informed decisions to be made about whether or not the placement should proceed. The first planning meeting sets the tone for introductions and it is therefore important that both current carers and new parents are involved and consulted. Effective chairing will ensure that different interests and perspectives are acknowledged and that agreement is reached regarding a plan that is centred on the child's needs while respecting those of the family. Ideally, the Chair will not have direct involvement in the placement and will bring skills that include mediating and negotiating as well as a thorough knowledge of child placement practice.

Planning meetings are not always comfortable or straightforward. Many feelings and expectations are in the room and it is sometimes a delicate process to work towards a mutually acceptable plan. Agencies may wish to consider ways in which they can help those involved prepare more carefully for these important decision-making stages. For example, one obvious way is to provide clear and detailed guidance about the purpose of the meeting(s) and an outline of a suggested format (see Tool 8). Another possibility is to produce an information leaflet explaining the principles of good practice that the agency feels are important in placing children. This could be adapted for different uses such as internal, interagency, and information for current and new carers, children/young people. Tensions in interagency work often arise as a result of different practice standards and expectations. The more prepared everyone can be from the earliest discussions about a placement, the better the chance of prompt resolution of difficulties and establishing positive working relationships.

A structure of planning meetings throughout the introductory period will enable those involved to review and monitor progress and to agree ongoing plans. While decisions need to be flexible and responsive to individual needs, it is not helpful to change plans arbitrarily. Clarity about the reason for planning meetings, their importance in the whole process and a commitment to working openly and in partnership, especially in the face of conflict or disagreement, are therefore important pre-conditions. One of the major anxieties for the child and new family (Lowe *et al*, 1999) is being clear about the purpose of introductions. While the shared hope is that a placement will be made, the reality is that introductions provide the opportunity for child and family to learn more about each other. By spending time together they begin to gain a sense of whether or not they may be able to live as a family and what this will mean.

But there remains the possibility that the child, family and/or agency may feel that placement is not the way forward. Doubts are not easy to voice at such emotionally demanding times. Yet introductions are not irrevocable and all involved need explicit permission to share reservations so that concerns can be aired and worked with. This may be painful but the alternatives can be far more damaging. Awareness of the added pressure of introducing potential parents as "Mum" and "Dad" (Lowe *et al*, 1999) may suggest that agencies need to give careful thought to how first introductions are made. Similarly, talking to children about "forever families" early in the process may cause increased confusion and hurt when introductions need to be halted. Sensitivity regarding age and levels of understanding is always paramount but most older children can appreciate that children and families need time to get to know each other and to think carefully about whether or not they can work at sharing their lives. Being explicit about the importance of taking the time to think, share, reflect and decide helps to establish a more realistic approach. In this way, uncertainties can be anticipated and expressed and the emotional pressure to agree to a placement for all the wrong reasons can be minimised. (For more information regarding Introductions see Smith, 1994, Chapter 5; Fahlberg, 1994, Chapter 4).

Communicating

One of the keys to successful introductions is often the capacity of the adults concerned to work together in the interests of the child. This is a time of great stress for all involved and each party, including the child, will have their own anxieties. Part of the professional role is to acknowledge this and contain it within a respectful and supportive process that aims to consider individual needs but with the interests of the child as its priority. This means acknowledging that adopters bring skills and knowledge to the placement process. Their experience of the child may be different from that of previous carers, as permanence brings with it a far more loaded emotional agenda. Listening to, reviewing with and empowering prospective adoptive parents will generally facilitate positive outcomes.

It is therefore important not to underestimate the contribution that good communication can make in easing the tensions inherent within introductions. Take the time to build rapport between potential new parent(s) and existing carers, birth family relatives, teachers, doctors and other involved professionals. Each of these important contacts will enable a new family to learn more about the child and to begin to build a picture of their needs. The temptation is to rush ahead with first meetings but once the family and child have met, another agenda opens up and the time and space for thinking and reflection are far harder to find. Taking time at the beginning of the process often allows adult fears to be addressed and dissipated, so leaving the face-to-face contact between child and family to focus on its primary aim of building and transferring attachments.

One obvious way of imparting information is for families to meet those people who know the child best. Social workers will hopefully be competent to paint an overall picture but the day-to-day detail will be best provided by meeting those involved. The timing of these various meetings will vary according to each case but care is necessary not to regard birth families as an afterthought. Their perspective, their lived experience with their children, and their capacity to give their child permission to make new relationships should not be underestimated. Meeting them sooner rather than later is an important part of understanding a child's history and is especially important if contact arrangements are part of the placement agreement. Similarly, siblings, their carers and other significant people in the child's life are also important people for new families to get to know prior to placement.

The views of children

Children express considerable anxiety about the introductory process, especially their expectations of both first and subsequent meetings (Thomas *et al*, 1999). In addition to the reassurance previously mentioned, children, like adults, need to understand in an age-appropriate way, the purpose of introductions and to be supported in dealing with the inevitable uncertainties. This is far from easy and much will depend on the age and understanding of the individual child. Yet it is tempting for the social worker to be over-optimistic about the future and if the match does not work the child's distress and confusion are even greater. Anxiety can be minimised by information, explanation, involvement in decisions that have been made and why, and rehearsing with the child the likely format of meetings, particularly the first.

This is a difficult time for all parties, and though stress will always be a part of introductions, good preparation can pay dividends. Openness about purpose together with shared planning about structure, activities, duration, who will be present, etc, can all help to ease the process. Just as potential parents want to know everything about the child so children also want to know as much as possible about their potential new family. Children find visual material especially helpful (Thomas *et al*, 1999) and creative thought needs to be given to how best to exchange information about lifestyle, family networks, neighbourhood, community, school, routines, interests and friendships. In several of the research studies (Thoburn *et al*, 1999; Thomas *et al*, 1999; Owen, 1999) children speak of the immense upheaval they have to face when joining new families. Social workers will want to consider with families how they can maintain children's existing important connections and more adequately prepare them for the changes ahead.

Timing and the use of time

Each child and family is unique and there can be no definitive answers to the question of how long introductions should take. Practice is informed by knowledge of child development and generally, the younger the child, the shorter and more intensive the introductory process. However, care should be taken not to collude with rushed arrangements; disruption experience as well as research (Lowe *et al*, 1999; Thomas *et al*, 1999) show that both children and adopters often feel that placements have been arranged too hurriedly. There may be good reasons for bringing forward a planned placement date, such as when both child and family feel ready and there is general agreement that to prolong introductions would serve no useful purpose. Yet other influences and pressures may result in precipitous action being taken that may not be in the interests of child or family.

One of the key factors in helping to assess the progress of introductions is how much quality time the child and family have spent together. The whole process may extend over some weeks, yet the amount of interaction between child and family and the child's familiarity with their proposed new lifestyle may be very limited. Interagency or long distance placements present particular challenges. The change of environment is even more marked for the child and all the usual family tensions are heightened by travel fatigue, emotional strain, isolation from friends and family and strange surroundings. While initial visits will normally take place on the child's familiar territory, once a rapport has been established it seems sensible to begin to move the focus to the family's environment. It is here that they will feel most comfortable, where the child will begin to piece together information and experience about family and community, and where ordinary opportunities for building relationships will be best provided.

External factors can sometimes exert a powerful influence on placement dates. School terms and holidays are the most common and while acknowledging the centrality of school in the lives of most children, it is only one of a number of important determinants. Holiday periods are favoured for arranging placements and may have real benefits. But additional strains can be created when child and family are faced with constant interaction for weeks on end, or when eagerly anticipated holidays are subject to the strains of incorporating a new family member. Holiday periods are also when many social workers and other professionals are on leave and child and family can find themselves with little or no support at this most vulnerable stage of the placement. Careful discussion of these issues and ensuring that appropriate support is in place can help to minimise the likelihood of problems undermining relationships from an early stage.

Special considerations

"Race" and culture

Children in public care and the families they are being placed with come from an increasingly diverse range of racial, cultural and religious backgrounds. Such diversity presents an additional challenge to placement practice as social workers strive to promote understanding and respect of differing values, practices and traditions. Planning for children involves careful assessment of the impact of their racial, cultural and religious identity and the implications this will have for placement with a new family.

Sadly, many children will not have had the opportunity to develop knowledge or experience of their backgrounds or traditions and will be disadvantaged as a result. It is simplistic to assume that to achieve a placement with families of the same heritage will provide the panacea for these children. They may be alienated from their ethnic/spiritual community, angry and confused about their identity, and subjected to a range of racial/religious abuse throughout their life. Much careful work is necessary in order to prepare not just the child but also the new family for the long-term implications of such a placement. (see Prevatt-Goldstein and Spencer, 2000; Smith, 1994, Chapter 4).

Disability

The implications of disability also need careful consideration during introductions. It is often difficult to convey to new families the complexities of a specific impairment and the implications for day-to-day care. Understanding the daily needs of severely disabled children will require intensive contact, first with existing carers whose experience and knowledge will be vital to share, and then with the child. Establishing communication through proximity, touch, language and play will facilitate the trust and rapport that precede the management of more intimate routines. It is often more important to give additional time to building relationships within the child's familiar setting before attempting to move into a different environment. Some disabled children may find this upsetting and disorientating and thus gradual, sensitive preparation will contribute towards a successful move. Disability is, of course, a broad spectrum and each child will respond differently depending on age, comprehension and individual needs. However, as a general rule, the time, preparation, quality of contact and management of transition that are key aspects of placement for every child will often require additional attention when disability is involved (see BAAF Practice Note 34).

Health and education

Every child has a medical history that is vital to share with prospective new families. In practice this assumes more importance when a child has a specific condition or when there are concerns about background. But detailed information covering the health history of every child and his/her family of origin is essential both to collate and to convey to new parents. Sometimes this is difficult to achieve but every effort should be made so that gaps or unanswered questions can be talked about fully when initial discussion takes place about the viability of the link. It is often most helpful for applicants to have the opportunity to meet the agency medical adviser, and in some cases they will need to discuss issues with other specialist staff. Interpreting medical information and its significance is an important aspect of understanding the needs of the child, and families need access to appropriate expertise in order to be adequately informed.

Many children moving into placement will have educational issues that require consideration and planning. Again, families need to be fully aware of the child's educational history and have the opportunity to discuss this with appropriate professionals and certainly to read and discuss educational assessments and statements. A shared approach is most helpful in finding the best school placement within the family's neighbourhood. Applicants can often make preliminary enquiries about what local resources can offer and sometimes will have much direct experience of different schools. But in addition, formal liaison between education departments is crucial to ensuring that the necessary official information is exchanged and that, with the family's involvement, the most suitable school can be identified.

Timing is not easy, especially when placements so often occur around holiday periods. It is therefore generally helpful for inter-school or departmental contact to take place sooner rather than later.

Placements made before school places are secured, unless specifically planned for good reasons, can place additional pressures on child and family and may result in long, stressful delays. The level of support and resources can vary considerably between areas and for some children this will be a key factor in deciding about placement. Social workers have important roles to play in co-ordinating the efforts of all involved to meet the individual needs of both child and family (see Jackson, forthcoming 2001).

Babies and toddlers

It is unwise to assume that baby placement is the "easy" end of the child placement spectrum. While it may be generally true that older children bring more complex experiences and behaviour patterns to their new families, there are also real issues to consider when placing infants and toddlers. The impact of violence, abuse, neglect and discontinuity of care cannot be ignored for any child and one of the most dangerous assumptions that social workers can make is to think that, because of their age, very young children must be less traumatised. This may be so if the child has experienced a protective and nurturing relationship in the midst of deprivation and risk; otherwise the implications of poor early care need both attention and remedial action.

Neither child nor family are helped if issues are minimised and social workers fail to provide families with a framework for making sense of attachment difficulties, their own responses and practical ways in which they can effect change (see Fahlberg, 1994; Archer, 1999a and b). Because small children are frequently placed quite quickly, the emotional preparation of new parents is a significant issue. Some will have waited for years, others may have only just been approved. Yet at very short notice they will be expected to leap into action and be practically and emotionally ready to receive someone else's baby or child into their care. For some, this adjustment will be dominated by the joy of parenting but for others the reality of managing the stresses involved may result in depression, guilt or panic. When this is compounded by attachment difficulties that make parents feel rejected or not needed, the pressures can become overwhelming. Both social workers and adopters need an awareness of how small children respond to separation, loss and trauma as well as the defensive strategies of the pre-verbal child. Every separated child will carry with them the hurt and pain of that initial loss (see Verrier, 1993) and for some this will involve sub-conscious trauma that may not emerge until much later. All this has important implications for preparation, post-approval support and development, careful, intensive introductions, and sensitive post-placement support.

Siblings

Introducing siblings to a new family, especially when they are in separate foster placements, will require extra time and planning. Prior to meeting a new family it will be important for the siblings to have spent as much time as possible together so that their own relationships, which so often diminish in separate placements, are given priority. Meeting the new family is important for siblings to do jointly but this may well need careful preparation to ensure that the family is not initially overwhelmed by differing needs. Structure and support will be invaluable as confidence in managing a group of needy children takes time and practice. It may occasionally be advisable to stagger the actual placement and older siblings can sometimes benefit from being placed first. This can give an element of security to the older child(ren), allow them to build their own rapport with the new parents and then play a key role in welcoming their younger siblings when appropriate.

But each situation is unique and for most family groups a joint placement will be the best plan. One of the most important aspects of introductions will often be the level of support available to each child and to the new family. Siblings are too often seen as one package whereas in reality each child has their own history (though much may be shared) and individual needs. Each will therefore need support in their own right and for new parents the task of making sense of their instant family and coping with the immense physical and emotional demands will be considerable. They will value a range of support services that might include social workers, experienced adopters, practical and financial help, and structured time out both for themselves and the children.

Reflecting and rehearsing

The impact of introducing a child to a potential new family cannot be underestimated. Strong emotions are involved and investments are high. Consequently,

it is vital that, in the midst of this emotional roller coaster, sufficient time and space is allowed for adequate reflection on how things are developing. The work that goes on in addition to the contacts between child and family, including the quality of communication between the respective social workers, is an essential tool in reviewing progress. It focuses on the early indicators of how this particular child "fits" within this particular family and both child and family need their own support workers to help them to honestly share feelings, hopes and fears. Families will change as a result of the incoming child's needs and all family members, including the children, will value the opportunity to reflect on the implications. Experienced adopters can also offer valuable support at this time and concerns or hesitations may be more readily shared with them than with professionals. It is, however, important that such discussions are fed back into the planning group so that open communication is maintained.

Introductions will also offer the chance for new family and child to "rehearse" different aspects of what living together will entail. Getting to know each other will involve sharing ordinary day-to-day routines, meeting family, friends, neighbours and just having fun together. Common interests can be a valuable focus in these early, tentative stages of relationship building and their importance should not be overlooked at the linking stage. The family will also begin to experience and manage the child's behaviours, bearing in mind earlier discussions that hopefully will have prepared them for any particular needs and considered strategies for responding. A careful visiting plan will gently expose the child to the family, their values, rules, roles, routines, and expectations, as well as how they express feelings, affection, and disapproval. This can best be achieved through visits that are not compressed into weekends or built around treats and outings. Family life is also about Monday to Friday, school, work, shopping, and making time and space for each other in the give and take of daily demands.

The more involved and prepared children can be to face the changes ahead, the more likely they are to make successful moves. Rehearsing aspects of their story and how they will explain their arrival to peers and new acquaintances will help them feel more confident in facing questions that otherwise can cause anxiety and embarrassment.

There is a degree to which introductions will always be artificial and the real work will not begin until placement and beyond. Yet these are life-changing events for those involved and it is important that while acknowledging the limitations, introductions are managed sensitively and efficiently. This is a critical first step for both child and family and the long-term implications are immense.

Supporting

Developing new attachments also implies letting go of previous ones and this is far from easy for children who may have had little experience of stability. It is important to acknowledge and accept their feelings of loss and sadness as well as their fears associated with leaving familiar people and places. All involved, especially the current foster carers, will need to be prepared to help the child to express and manage these feelings. The foster carers' support for both the child and new family throughout introductions is crucial and the importance of the foster carers' contribution is recognised in research (Lowe *et al*, 1999). The child will need permission and reassurance in order to feel free to emotionally disengage and move on. Where possible, birth family members can also make a significant contribution. Their involvement in the linking process and their knowledge and acceptance of the new family can minimise the danger of divided loyalties for the child. But the reality of introductions can be stressful for all involved and both birth relatives and foster families will need support in their own right in order to deal with their feelings while giving priority to the interests of the child.

In the same way, individual support for the child should be a natural continuation of the direct work that has helped prepare him/her for placement and that will hopefully be available throughout. Children will have many emotions to deal with at this time and need the opportunity to express their feelings. Managing the reality of loss – of their birth family, their current family and most, if not all, of their familiar daily routines – along with the hopes and fears about the new family and the future it

symbolises is far from easy. Support for the child is a crucial part of introduction work, and listening to his/her views and observing play and behaviour will provide important evidence about the child's readiness to move on.

Last but not least, social workers also need their own support systems throughout what can be a delicate and demanding phase of trying to take account of the wishes and feelings of the various parties and reach agreement about the way forward. Social workers will often have strong emotional connections with their child or family. They will need and value the opportunity for ongoing communication throughout introductions, and regular reviews can help to avoid the escalation of potential difficulties. The availability of an objective ear is also vital, whether this is achieved through supervision and/or ongoing liaison with family placement team workers. Agencies need to consider how, within their structures and policies, specialist knowledge can best be shared for the benefit of all involved.

Introductions – summary

● Structure planning meetings to enable ongoing sharing, review and joint decision making.

● Ensure that child and family receive regular support and permission to air concerns; remember the support needs of current foster families and birth relatives.

● Take the time to build adult rapport and give new parents every opportunity to form an accurate picture of the child's needs.

● Involve the child in plans for introductions and clarify purpose and process.

● Aim to plan visits that allow increasing time together in the family's environment.

● Try to be less influenced by external factors than by what seems right for child and family.

● Discuss child's networks and relationships with new family and clarify plans for contact well in advance.

5 Moving in

The final planning meeting will review the introductory period, come to a decision about a placement date, and confirm the details of the placement agreement. This is important in terms of clarifying roles, responsibilities and expectations around such issues as social work involvement, contact, finance, support services, multidisciplinary liaison, etc – all of which should have been thoroughly explored from an early stage.

Managing the move appropriately is important for everybody but especially the child. Many will have had multiple moves and carers in their short lives, often resulting in confusion, fear and insecurity. This move needs to be seen and experienced differently. If introductions have worked well, the child will gradually have been letting go of his/her current world and preparing to invest in the new family and their networks. This will involve saying goodbye to significant others such as teachers, classmates, friends and clubs. While goodbyes are important, it is also necessary to be sensitive about the impact of prolonged and repeated farewells on children who are inevitably anxious about taking new risks. A small family party arranged by the foster carers, and perhaps involving adopters, which gives various people the opportunity to wish the child well is one solution. Successive farewells close to the moving date, particularly when they include birth relatives, can place immense pressure on the child and may leave little emotional energy to deal with the actual move and initial adjustment.

The aim of the introductory process is to test out the viability of the proposed placement and, once agreed, to ensure a sensitive transition for the child. Throughout the process, both child and family have been building information and experience about each other and, once the moving date is confirmed, it can be helpful to consolidate this in a concrete way. Children can be anxious about what families do or do not know about their history and it can often be useful to encourage an open sharing of the past, perhaps with the help of a life story book or other visual aids. The child may well need support in order to revisit painful memories but the affirmation received from the family can offer relief and reassurance. The messages conveyed to the child are that it is safe to talk about the past and about

feelings, that the family knows about and accepts both them and their story, and that they remain committed to working together at becoming a family. This can be a powerful and symbolic way of reviewing and sharing the past in order to look positively, yet realistically, to the future.

Contact

Another anxiety that children will have around placement concerns contact with significant people in their life. Much discussion will have taken place with the new family about the child's networks and important relationships. It is important that everyone, especially the child, is clear about arrangements for contact, whether direct or indirect. Children in public care have often had many moves and repeated losses. Continuity is something they rarely experience and current practice needs to be more alert to the importance of maintaining positive contacts where possible. There may be sound reasons for not supporting certain contact arrangements but there will always be some significant people who can help the child to affirm their identity and history.

This range of people might include birth relatives, siblings, previous carers, friends, and social workers, and will vary according to individual circumstances. What seems important is that thought is given to the child's important connections and how best they can be sustained for the benefit of both child and family. Certainly most children will want to maintain some contact with their foster carers, at least in the short term, and it is worrying how many lose touch so quickly after placement. A supportive visit from the previous carer during the early part of the placement that focuses on the present and future can often reassure the child.

Yet practice often reflects social work concerns that such contacts may be undermining and that both physical and emotional distance are necessary in order to enable new relationships to flourish. This reasoning ignores what we know about child development, loss and grief, and places children, and their families, in situations of confusion and risk. The determining factor would seem to be the capacity of the visitor to actively support and encourage the new placement. When this is the case and the child has been well prepared, ongoing contacts can be beneficial for all parties (see BAAF Good Practice Guide, 1999).

Support

After placement, the value of support for child and family is paramount as they confront the reality of living together and the ongoing adjustment that will be necessary. The first step towards building lasting attachments is for the child to feel safe and contained, whatever their age. In these early days it is therefore important to support the family in giving clear messages to the child that reinforce their security. Familiar routines, especially for young and disabled children, are generally helpful to maintain initially; boundaries need to be clearly defined and consistency will be a key parenting quality. The child will be processing innumerable changes along with mixed emotions. Adults need to respond with both warmth and sensitivity to these demands as well as demonstrating that they are in control.

For infants and very young children the emphasis will also be on safety but alongside the close daily contact that facilitates attachments. This will be an important factor for both social worker and new family to recognise, as early intervention can have such positive benefits for both child and adult. Many interactions will come naturally but reinforcing the importance of smell, touch, physical proximity, individual time and appropriate play will encourage new parents to attend to their child's sensory development and be proactive in sensitively initiating attachment behaviours when appropriate.

Many children and families will require a broad range of support services. Hopefully these will have been identified and discussed at the earliest stages of linking and certainly at the first introduction planning meeting. It is important that measures to put such supports in place are taken sooner rather than later. Disruption experience shows that possible avenues of support are often mentioned during introductions but that a "let's wait and see" approach is taken. When there are strong indications that support such as therapeutic services and respite care may be needed, it is worthwhile locating such resources as soon as possible and prior to placement. They may not be needed, but if they are they can be mobilised quickly and their contribution may make all the difference. While accepting the limitations of local resources in some areas, children and families are often struggling for too long with immense stress without the appropriate help.

Social workers can only do so much but it is vital that they are experienced and equipped to provide a knowledgeable and quality service. Agencies, their panels and, encouragingly, the latest Government consultation document (PIU, 2000) increasingly recognise the obligation to offer an ongoing post-placement service that genuinely supports parents in caring for hurt and vulnerable children. Existing adopters have much to offer in this respect and local efforts to maximise their commitment and experience can provide invaluable networks of support and encouragement.

Moving in – summary

- Plan the final move carefully with all involved and try to minimise additional emotional pressures on the child.

- Consider overtly sharing child's history between child and family prior to placement and using this as an opportunity for mutual commitment.

- Discuss early post-placement contacts and how they can best be managed.

- Work closely with child and family on initial adjustment phase – lay foundations for ongoing support.

- Ensure that support systems are alerted prior to placement so that if needed they can be mobilised promptly.

6 Conclusion

Placing children with new families is a complex task that has to take account of many different needs and interests. This Practice Guide can only hope to highlight some of the main areas that social workers may find helpful to address. But each child and family is unique and there is no concrete formula that can be rigidly applied. Recent research has increased awareness of certain issues but it is true that many of the resulting suggestions are simply basic good practice. The reality is that, as a result of widespread organisational changes, many social service departments have lost their child placement expertise at a time when there is an unparalleled focus on the value of adoption for some children. This Practice Guide aims to offer a framework for thinking more carefully about the social work role in linking and introductions but it cannot be a substitute for the training, supervision and ongoing development that is essential to providing quality services to children and families.

Important messages for policy and practice

Key messages for adults supporting children through the adoption process include the need for them to:

- express themselves simply and clearly when communicating with children about adoption and to match their explanations of new ideas to the children's ages and levels of understanding;

- be aware of the possible impact of emotional distress on children's understanding;

- offer reassurances and encouragement to children about their moves to their adoptive homes;

- try to match the pace of change to the child's pace of change;

- prepare children carefully for court;

- use robust materials for making life-story books;

- plan for the revision and up-dating of life-story work;

- take into account children's powerful and changing wishes and feelings about contact when making contact arrangements;

- keep contact arrangements under review; and

- be sensitive to children's feelings about others knowing that they are adopted.

(Extracted from *Adoption Now: Messages from Research*, 1999)

7 References

Archer C (1999a) *First Steps in Parenting the Child Who Hurts*, London: Jessica Kingsley.

Archer C (1999b) *Next Steps in Parenting the Child Who Hurts*, London: Jessica Kingsley.

BAAF (1997) Practice Note 34 *The Placement of Children with Disabilities*, London: BAAF.

BAAF (1999) Good Practice Guide *Contact in Permanent Placement: guidance for local authorities in England and Wales and Scotland*, London: BAAF.

Dartington Social Research Unit (1995) *Child Protection: Messages from Research*, London: HMSO.

DoH (2000) *Framework for the Assessment of Children in Need and their Families*, London: The Stationery Office.

DoH Circular LAC 98 (20) *Achieving the Right Balance*, London: Department of Health.

Fahlberg V (1994) *A Child's Journey through Placement*, London: BAAF.

Jackson S (ed) (2001, forthcoming) *Nobody Told Us School Mattered: The educational attainment of children in care*, London: BAAF.

Kirton D and Woodger D (1999) 'Experiences of transracial adoption' in *Assessment, Preparation and Support: Implications from research*, London: BAAF.

Lord J, Barker S and Cullen D (2000) *Effective Panels* (2nd edn), London: BAAF.

Lord J and Borthwick S (2001, forthcoming) *Together or Apart? Assessing brothers and sisters for permanent placement*, London: BAAF.

Lowe N, Murch M, Borkowski M, Weaver A, Beckford V and Thomas C (1999) *Supporting Adoption: Reframing the Approach*, London: BAAF.

Owen M (1999) *Novices, Old Hands and Professionals: Adoption by single people*, London: BAAF.

Parker R (ed) (1999) *Adoption Now: Messages from Research*, Chichester: Wiley.

Performance and Innovation Unit (PIU) Report (2000) *Prime Minister's Review of Adoption*, London: PIU.

Phillips R and McWilliam E (eds) (1996) *After Adoption: Working with adoptive families*, London: BAAF.

Prevatt Goldstein B and Spencer M (2000) *"Race" and Ethnicity: Consideration of issues for black, minority ethnic and white children in family placement*, London: BAAF.

Quinton D, Rushton A, Dance C and Mayes D (1998) *Joining New Families: A study of adoption and fostering in middle childhood*, Chichester: Wiley.

Rutter M and the ERA team (1998) 'Developmental catch-up and deficit following adoption after severe global early privation', *J Child Psychol Psychiat*, 39: 465-76.

Schofield G (1998) 'Making sense of the ascertainable wishes and feelings of insecurely attached children', *Child and Family Law Quarterly*, Vol 10:4.

Sellick C and Thoburn J (1997) *What Works in Family Placement*, Essex: Barnardo's.

Smith S (1994) *Learning from Disruption: Making better placements*, London: BAAF.

Thoburn J, Norford L and Rashid S (1999) 'Permanent family placement of children of minority ethnic origin' in Parker R (1999) *Adoption Now: Messages from Research*, Chichester: Wiley.

Thomas C and Beckford V with Murch M and Lowe N (1999) *Adopted Children Speaking*, London: BAAF.

Verrier N (1993) *The Primal Wound*, Baltimore: Gateway Press, USA.

Wedge P and Mantle G (1991) *Sibling Groups in Social Work*, Aldershot: Avebury.

Resources

Useful reading for new workers in different aspects of family placement

Planning

BAAF Good Practice Guide (1999) *Contact in Permanent Placement*, London: BAAF

BAAF Practice Note 33 *Planning for Permanence*, London: BAAF

Working with Children and Young People

Barn R (ed) (1999) *Working with Black Children and Adolescents in Need*, London: BAAF

Ryan T and Walker R (1999) *Life Story Work*, London: BAAF

Fahlberg V (1994) *A Child's Journey through Placement*, London: BAAF

Jewitt C (1995) *Helping Children cope with Separation and Loss*, London: Batsford

Gilligan R (2000) *Promoting Resilience: A resource guide for working with children in care*, London: BAAF

Prevatt-Goldstein B and Spencer M (2000) *"Race" and Ethnicity: A consideration of issues for black, minority ethnic and white children in family placement*, BAAF Good Practice Guide, London: BAAF

Turning Points – A Resource Pack for Communicating with Children (1997) London: NSPCC

Siblings

Borthwick S and Lord J (forthcoming, 2001) *Together or Apart? Assessing brothers and sisters for permanent placement*, London: BAAF

Mullender A (ed) (1999) *We are Family*, London: BAAF

Disability

Argent H and Kerrane A (1997) *Taking Extra Care*, London: BAAF

Education

Jackson S (ed) (forthcoming, 2001) *No one told us school mattered*, London: BAAF

Preparation, Assessment and Support of Applicants

BAAF (1999) *Making Good Assessments – A Practical Resource Guide*, London: BAAF

Phillips R and McWilliam E (eds) (1996) *After Adoption*, London: BAAF

Useful addresses

Adoption UK (formerly PPIAS)
Lower Boddington, near Daventry
Northamptonshire NN11 6YB
Tel: 01327 260295

BAAF Head Office
Skyline House, 200 Union Street
London SE1 0LX
Tel: 020 7593 2000

National Foster Care Association (NFCA)
87 Blackfriars Road, London SE1 8HA
Tel: 020 7620 6400

Tools

Permanency Planning Options
Agenda for Permanency Planning Meetings
The Assessment Framework
Matching Meeting Agenda
Matching report Outline
Matching Criteria
Child Appreciation Days
Introductions Planning Meeting Agenda
Adoption Flow Chart

1 Permanency planning options

The first consideration must be the ability of the child's family of origin to provide safe, permanent care for the child, and for this to be achieved within a reasonable period of time. If and when this option has been ruled out, consideration must be given to each alternative legal route to secure the child's future care.

Checklist of indicators for permanency planning

Adoption	Long-term fostering	Residence order
Primary need is for the child to "belong" to a family who will make a lifelong commitment.	Primary need is for a significant level of continued involvement with the child's birth family.	The child needs the security of a legally defined placement with alternative carers, but does not require a lifelong commitment involving a change of identity.
The birth parents are not able or not willing to share parental responsibility in order to meet the child's needs, even though there may be contact.	The child's sense of belonging is catered for by the birth family, so that the child has a clear sense of identity whilst needing to be looked after by another family.	The carer needs to exercise day-to-day parental responsibility
The child needs an opportunity to develop a new sense of identity whilst being encouraged to maintain a healthy understanding of his/her past.	There is a need for continuing oversight, monitoring and review of the child's welfare in the placement.	There is no need for continuing oversight, monitoring and review by the local authority.
The child expresses a wish to be adopted.	Birth parents are able and willing to exercise a degree of parental responsibility.	

* "Belonging" refers to the child's ability to develop and sustain a sense of security, identity and self-esteem in the context of a stable, healthy attachment.

Reproduced with permission from Devon Social Services.

2 Sample agenda for permanency planning meetings

1 Use CHECKLIST FOR REFERRING A CHILD FOR PERMANENCY (Guidance Note 1) – go through and identify missing information.

2 At the first P.P.M. discussion must be held about whether family finding is appropriate for the child at this time. PERMANENCY TEAM MANAGER TO RECORD THIS TEAM'S ACCEPTANCE OF REFERRAL FOR FAMILY FINDING.

3 Assess/confirm placement needs of child (Guidance Note 3).

4 Copy of *Looking After Children: Assessment and Action Record* to be given to family finder.

5 Identify work that needs to be done with child at all stages.

6 Clarify/review who is best placed to prepare child for new placement (NB this should involve some skills in direct work with children):

- Child's social worker (may not be appropriate if he/she has "removed" child from birth family and may still be working with the birth family)

- Foster carer's linkworker

- Family finder or residential worker in conjunction with any of the above

- Specialist worker e.g. play therapist (funding will need to be addressed).

7 Identify any possible approved family (or in pipeline, i.e. being assessed). If no family available, see Guidance Note 9 (Advertising) and prepare workers for work involved.

8 If child has very special needs, clarify if/when referral for family finding to outside agency may be appropriate and identify budget for this.

9 Identify work with birth family and who should undertake this (Guidance Note 10).

10 Decision about whether an adoption allowance is to be requested (Guidance Note 8).

11 Legal issues (e.g. (i) has case been discussed with Legal Section

                (ii) consideration of freeing for adoption.

12 Wishes of birth parents re: involvement in family finding process/future meetings.

13 Birth parents' views/agreement for potential publicity of their child, including use of photographs. NB. For local and national press advertising, TV or internet, permission from parent(s) is required.

Reproduced with permission from Hillingdon Social Services.

3 The assessment framework

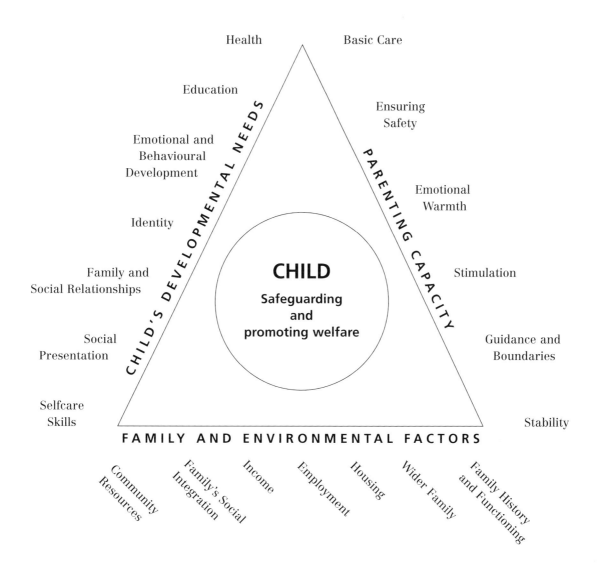

Health   Basic Care

Education

CHILD'S DEVELOPMENTAL NEEDS

Emotional and
Behavioural
Development

PARENTING CAPACITY

Ensuring
Safety

Identity

Emotional
Warmth

CHILD
Safeguarding
and
promoting welfare

Family and
Social Relationships

Stimulation

Social
Presentation

Guidance and
Boundaries

Selfcare
Skills

Stability

FAMILY AND ENVIRONMENTAL FACTORS

Community
Resources   Family's Social
Integration   Income   Employment   Housing   Wider Family   Family History
and Functioning

Extracted from 'Framework for the Assessment of Children in Need and their Families', Department of Health, 2000.

4 Matching meeting: sample agenda

Chaired by AFU Co-Ordinator/AFU Family Finder

1   Update on current situation. Any changes? How is/are the child/ren?

2   Clarify legal issues. (Checklist: eg freeing, change of name, contact, legal status, parental agreement.)

3   Health. Are medicals up to date? Any health issues?

4   Review child's Profile of Needs. Which of these are essential, which are desired?

5   Look in detail at all families being considered and share experience of visits.

6   Decide whether any of these families meet the children's needs and would be suitable placements.

7   **If no family is suitable**

Decide next steps (visit other families waiting, re-advertise, etc).

Fix date for next meeting and decide who should be invited.

8   **If a match is agreed**

Points for consideration

    a)   How and when family are informed of matching and by whom.

    b)   Consider Matching Report [see Sample Matching Report, page 25].

    c)   Issues around Adoption Allowance (if agreed)/Fostering Allowance.
       Is family expecting an allowance? If so, has a Statement of Income been completed?
       For fostering, do we need to look at enhancement?

Reproduced with permission from Wandsworth Social Services.

5 Sample matching report

Proposed placement for adoption or fostering

Purpose

To provide the Panel with up-to-date but comprehensive information about the child's needs and the potential of the proposed family to meet those needs. The matching report needs to emphasise the opportunities and the issues for the child in becoming part of this new family, so that the issues can be considered and assessed by the Panel.

Timing of report

The matching report should be prepared in the light of:

a) Full interagency consultation, the exchange of written reports (Form E and F, medical educational reports, court orders).

b) The child's social worker meeting the prospective family and furnishing them with written information regarding the child's history and needs and identifying with the family any areas for further work with the child.

c) Clarification of financial support to the placement and a written plan for interagency working.

d) The informed decision of the proposed family to proceed to Panel.

Format of the report

1. *The child's needs*
   (For sibling groups to be placed together, this checklist should be considered separately for each child.)

   a) **Pen picture** – physical description, temperament and current behaviour.

   b) **Geographical considerations** – such as need for contact, friendships and sense of identity.

   c) **Medical** – genetic considerations and current health.

   d) **Ethnic** – cultural origins and experience.

   e) **Religion** – birth parents' wishes must be considered.

   f) **Legal** – current legal status – existing orders. Possibility of future contested cases over adoption, contact, etc. Legal adviser's opinion.

   g) **Educational** – already identified, e.g. statement of educational need or prospective needs.

   h) **Lifestyle** – including experiences in care – relevant to older children.

   i) **Emotional needs** – e.g. adjustment to past changes, relationships with adults/carers/peers.

   j) **Sibling relationships** – where children are to be placed together.

   k) **"Telling"** – facts about family of origin. Reasons for separation, history in care. Implications of these for children in future. How the child has coped. What preparation/life story work has taken place?

   l) **Contact** – current agreement for contact. Implications for this for birth family members (including siblings, if separated).

   m) **Finance** – eligibility for adoption allowance or additional and exceptional settling-in allowances, adaptations to property required.

   n) **The child's wishes and feelings** – about the plan, the type of family.

2. *Wishes of the birth parents* (separately as necessary)

Regarding:

   a) Family composition of placement family

   b) Initial meeting

   c) Future contact.

3. *Family finding efforts undertaken*

Any other families considered and the reasons for not pursuing a match with them.

4. *Capacity of proposed family to parent this child or children*

   a) The strengths the family has to meet the needs of the child or children, as described above.

   b) Special skills available to meet exceptional needs in family and in support network.

   c) The family's capacity to meet the needs of each child in a sibling group and the combined needs of the group.

   d) The family's attitude to the particular background circumstances. The personal strengths and practical resources available to deal with contact.

   e) The resources of other family members, such as other children and grandparents, to meet the child or children's identified needs.

5. *Areas where the proposed family will need support*

As perceived and made explicit by the child's agency, the family and the family's agency.

   a) Projected areas of difficulty, in the short- or longer-term, or times of particular sensitivity in the child's or the family's future development.

   b) The support available from each agency in the post-placement and, if applicable, post-adoption period, to deal with projected and unforeseen difficulties.

   c) The family's attitude to agency support.

Recommendation and any other comments

Such as proposed timing and timescale of introductions and practical considerations.
Reasons to give weight to this recommendation.

Reproduced with permission from Barnardo's Jigsaw Project.

6 Sample matching criteria

Please indicate the extent to which each family meets this child's needs:
**completely   *adequately   – unable   (to be added during matching meeting)

Child's social worker to complete		Family Placement Team workers to complete		
Needs to be met	Essential/preferable	Family 1	Family 2	Family 3
1. Ethnicity				
2. Culture				
3. Religion				
4. Language				
5. Attachment				
6. Challenging behaviour				
7. Personality				
8. Health				
9. Disability				
10. Education				
11. Status in family (e.g. eldest/only)				
12. Physical characteristics/ appearance				
13. Child's wishes				
14. Birth parent's wishes				
15. Interests/Hobbies/Talents				
16. Contact/Postbox				
17. Location				
18. Other – Specify				

1. This criteria is to form the basis of your discussion with potential adopters during your home visit.
2. This form should also be used to write your matching report after the matching meeting and before Panel attendance.

Reproduced with permission from Bristol Social Services.

7 Information on child appreciation days

Why hold a Child Appreciation Day?

Working with adopters/long-term foster carers and children has taught us an important lesson. We realise that we have not been doing enough to make the children we place come alive as "flesh and blood" people before they meet our carers.

In the past, after a placement has broken down and when a Disruption Meeting is held, carers and workers have heard information not previously known. The reasons for this knowledge being lost or unavailable may have been

- because the worker who knew the child earlier in his or her life has moved on and information that seemed less important at the time was stored only in that worker's memory

- or that people who had intimate knowledge of the child's personality and reactions to events were not asked to make personal recordings of their impressions.

Most importantly, however, often it is that we as adults have failed to enter into the mind and feelings of the child and their lives and experiences have been recorded in adult's words and concepts that turned the child into a "proper" profile.

The aim of a Child Appreciation Day is to bring alive the child for the people who will be making a relationship with him/her and who will be helping them make sense of their past.

On a Child Appreciation Day, we try to introduce to our adopters/permanent foster carers the people who, although they might be involved in a "conventional" planning meeting for a child, nevertheless have significant personal knowledge of the child (e.g., the nursery nurse; the health visitor; the relative who might have tried to give support). These people often have important recollections to share with adopters. Clearly we cannot ask everyone to help as limitations of time and considerations of confidentiality have to be taken into account. The presence of present carers is very important.

When should a Child Appreciation Day be held?

Once a match between a child and family has been agreed by both Barnardo's Panel and the local authority panel, we suggest a Life Appreciation Day should be planned to take place before or during the introductory period so the prospective carers begin the placement with as full a picture as possible about the child who is joining their family.

The day can also highlight information which may assist in the planning of the move into placement or the support which may be needed by the child and family following the beginning of the placement.

There may be situations where a child is already in placement and a Child Appreciation Day could be usefully held to assist carers/professionals in gaining a clearer understanding of the child's past.

Who should attend?

- Prospective adopters/foster carers
- Family's link worker
- Present foster carers/residential workers
- Child's social worker

- Previous social workers

- Previous foster carers

- Teacher

- Previous teachers

- Nursery/Family centre workers/Playscheme workers

- Health visitors

- Family members/extended family members – where appropriate

- Any other involved adults

Planning for the day

- The child's social worker will be asked to liaise with [the Barnardo's Jigsaw Worker] re: invitation list, and invites will be sent out as early as possible.

- A venue will be agreed and booked, preferably in the geographical area where the child is currently placed to facilitate attendance of involved adults.

- The child's agency will be asked to arrange lunch for participants.

- The social worker will need to prepare a family tree and a flow chart of significant events/moves in the child's life. These should be sent to the Senior/Project Leader facilitating the day with the Form E and any other relevant documents, preferably a week before the Child Appreciation Day.

- Attendees should read up on any files/diaries/records about the child before the day and bring along any photos/memorabilia which could be passed on to the new carers.

- The Child Appreciation Day will usually take place over four to five hours with a break for lunch.

- Ideally, the day will be run sequentially and most participants benefit from attending all day, as it is by hearing other people's contributions that thoughts and memories are activated. However, recognising that people may have time constraints, it is possible to enable them to have a "slot" during the day.

What happens during the Child Appreciation Day?

The leader of the Child Appreciation Day takes participants on a conducted journey through the life of the child, particularly searching for clues about experiences that occurred when paper knowledge was sketchy. A family tree will be drawn up at the beginning of the day and usually a flow chart drawn up.

Reproduced with permission from Barnardo's Jigsaw Project.

8 Sample agenda for introductions planning meeting

N.B. Preferably before this meeting

i) **All attending should be given an extract to read from Vera Fahlberg's *Helping Children When They Must Move**:**

    i)   "Helping a pre-verbal child move into adoption" or

    ii) "Helping a verbal child move into adoption", as appropriate.

ii) **For interagency placements**

    i)   Hold interagency meeting for completion of BAAF Form H1.

    ii) Form H2 can be partially completed prior to the introductions planning meeting, to save time, and largely overlaps with the content of this guidance note.

1 Give out to everyone:

i) Checklist for introduction of child to adoptive family

ii) Timetable sheets.

2 Any outstanding matters arising from previous Permanency Planning Meeting? – e.g. life history work/book; provision of background information; health reports on child.

3 *Statutory notifications*

Family placement team (FPT) administrator to send these out to:
    i)   Prospective adopters' local authority SSD
    ii)   Health authority
    iii) New GP
    iv) Family Finder or social worker (SW) to inform health visitor (adopters to find out who this is) of date on which placement with adopters has been confirmed, requesting health visitor visit a.s.a.p. after this.
    v)   FPT administrator to send statutory notification of panel's decision re: matching child with prospective adopters to
        i)   birth parents
        ii) adopters
    vi) Adopters to respond to above letter in writing
    vii) Interagency forms to be completed/signed/copied as appropriate.

4 *Equipment/Introduction costs and payments*

Clarify agreed costs, i.e.
– Payment towards equipment
– Transport costs during introductions
– Fostering allowance/adoption allowance: clarify how much and when to start/end; bank details to be completed by prospective adopters and passed to FPT administrator.
– What items will go with child? (e.g. clothes/bedding/toys/bottles/dummies/ special items such as hospital cot tags, first clothes, hair snippet etc.)

NB. Cot mattresses should not be used for different foster children (DoH guidance), so consider this going with child to new placement.

* This is now available within *A Child's Journey through Placement*, BAAF, 1994.

5 *Contact*

- One-off meeting with birth parent(s) or others? When? Where? Who will facilitate?
- Letterbox contact – With whom? Who will make arrangements?
- Initial/ongoing contact between adopters and foster carers post-placement.
- Direct contact with anyone?
- Is anyone else important in child's life?

6 *Support*

Clarify respective roles re: placement supervision/support.

i)   Agency support
- for child: (SW); who in SW's absence? (e.g. line manager)
- emergency duty team telephone number.
- for adopters – (linkworker); who in linkworker's absence? (e.g. line manager)
- for foster carers – (linkworker); who in absence? (e.g. adopter's linkworker/line manager)

ii) Informal support; from foster carers to adopters – What are the expectations?

7 *Reviews*

i)   Of introductions: to be built into introduction programme.

ii) Statutory reviews: to be held after one month; three months; then six-monthly (minimum).

iii) Where to be held?

iv) Who to arrange?

8 *Introductions*

- General issues, e.g. applicants' work commitments; does anybody have to work a period of notice?; availability of both applicants in daytime/evenings; any period when unavailable?
- State general time-frame envisaged for introductions.
- Stress need for this to go at child's pace.
- Review of introductions meeting will confirm anticipated date.
- For an older child, where introductions are likely to be over a more lengthy period of time, it is probably appropriate to plan a detailed introduction programme only as far as the review. It is also less appropriate to use the "timetable" sheets.

9 *Introductions programme*

- Ensure a social worker from Hillingdon is present when adopters first meet with child.
- Draw up in detail.
- Decide who is responsible for drawing up/circulating a "master copy" (usually Family Finder).

10 Confirm actions.

11 Confirm who will type up/circulate minutes to all a.s.a.p.

Reproduced with permission from Hillingdon Social Services.

9 Adoption Flow Chart

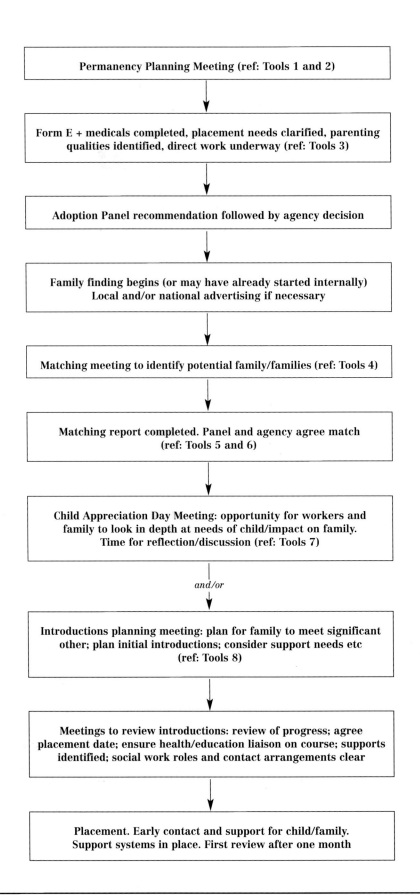

Permanency Planning Meeting (ref: Tools 1 and 2)

↓

Form E + medicals completed, placement needs clarified, parenting qualities identified, direct work underway (ref: Tools 3)

↓

Adoption Panel recommendation followed by agency decision

↓

Family finding begins (or may have already started internally) Local and/or national advertising if necessary

↓

Matching meeting to identify potential family/families (ref: Tools 4)

↓

Matching report completed. Panel and agency agree match (ref: Tools 5 and 6)

↓

Child Appreciation Day Meeting: opportunity for workers and family to look in depth at needs of child/impact on family. Time for reflection/discussion (ref: Tools 7)

and/or

↓

Introductions planning meeting: plan for family to meet significant other; plan initial introductions; consider support needs etc (ref: Tools 8)

↓

Meetings to review introductions: review of progress; agree placement date; ensure health/education liaison on course; supports identified; social work roles and contact arrangements clear

↓

Placement. Early contact and support for child/family. Support systems in place. First review after one month